The Lift-Your-Spirits Quote Book

Compiled by
Allen Klein

Gramercy Books
New York

For my mother-in-law Betty,
who has always
kept her spirits high.

This 2001 edition is published by Gramercy Books™,
an imprint of Random House Value Publishing, Inc.,
280 Park Avenue, New York, New York 10017.

Gramercy Books™ and design are trademarks of
Random House Value Publishing, Inc.

Random House
New York • Toronto • London • Sydney • Auckland
http://www.randomhouse.com/

Designer: Karen Ocker

Printed and bound in Singapore

Library of Congress Cataloging-in-Publication Data

The lift-your-spirits quote book / compiled by Allen Klein.
        p. cm.
    Includes index.
      ISBN 0-517-16309-8
      1. Happiness—Quotations, maxims, etc. 2. Consolation—Quotations, maxims, etc.
    I. Klein, Allen.

PN 6084.H3 L54 2000
170—dc21   00-047622

8 7 6 5 4 3 2 1

CONTENTS

INTRODUCTION

Psychoneuroimmunology is a long word with a short, simple concept. It means that the body, mind, and spirit are interconnected. In other words, your mind can influence your body. What you think affects how you feel. Of course, what you think consists mainly of words—and those words have the power to drag you down or lift you up.

The quotations in this book were all selected to help you experience the latter. To get the full effect, try posting a few where you will see them regularly. Add one a day to the screen saver on your computer, put one at the end of your E-mails, or E-mail one daily to someone whose spirit needs a lift.

It almost doesn't matter how you use these quotes. The important thing is that you use them on a regular basis. If you do, they can help keep your spirits high so that you will be mentally, physically, and spiritually healthier.

Allen Klein
San Francisco

**A powerful agent
is the right word.**

MARK TWAIN

Applause

Arts

Art ✶ Dance ✶ Music ✶ Poetry

When someone does something well, applaud!
You will make two people happy.

SAMUEL GOLDWYN

He who praises another enriches himself far more than
he does the one praised. To praise is an investment in
happiness. The poorest human being has something to
give that the richest could not buy.

GEORGE MATTHEW ADAMS

The way to develop the best that is in a man
is by appreciation and encouragement.

CHARLES SCHWAB

The applause of a single human being is of great consequence.

SAMUEL JOHNSON

Most people like praise . . . When it is really deserved,
most people expand under it into richer and better selves.

JOSEPH FARRELL

The sweetest of all sounds is praise.

XENOPHON

Down deep we really know our worth, but we don't have easy access to that knowledge. We need to hear praise coming from outside ourselves or we won't remember that we deserve it.

BARBARA SHER

Find the good—and praise it.

ALEX HALEY

Every day, tell at least one person something you like, admire, or appreciate about them.

RICHARD CARLSON

Judicious praise is to children what the sun is to flowers.

CHRISTIAN BOVEE

A little praise
Goes a great ways.

RALPH WALDO EMERSON

Art is much less important than life,
but what a poor life without it.

ROBERT MOTHERWELL

Art washes away from the soul the dust of everyday life.

PABLO PICASSO

Without art, the crudeness of reality
would make the world unbearable.

GEORGE BERNARD SHAW

Art is a staple, like bread or wine or a warm coat in winter.
Man's spirit grows hungry for art in the same way
his stomach growls for food.

IRVING STONE

The object of art is to give life a shape.

JEAN ANOUILH

The artist has a special task and duty; the task of reminding
men of their humanity and the promise of their creativity.

LEWIS MUMFORD

Each of us is an artist, capable of conceiving
and creating a vision from the depths of our being.

DOROTHY FADIMAN

All that is good in art is the expression of one soul talking to another;
and is precious according to the greatness of the soul that utters it.

JOHN RUSKIN

The artist alone sees spirits. But after he has told
of their appearing to him, everybody sees them.

GOETHE

Artists are nearest God. Into their souls he breathes his life, and from
their hands it comes in fair, articulate forms to bless the world.

JOSIAH GILBERT HOLLAND

A work of art has an author and yet, when it is perfect,
it has something which is anonymous about it.

SIMONE WEIL

The true work of art is but a shadow of the divine perfection.

MICHELANGELO

The artist is the confidant of nature, flowers carry on dialogues
with him through the graceful bending of their stems and the
harmoniously tinted nuances of their blossoms. Every flower
has a cordial word which nature directs towards him.

AUGUSTE RODIN

There are painters who transform the sun to a yellow spot,
but there are others who with the help of their art
and their intelligence, transform a yellow spot into sun.

PABLO PICASSO

Science and art have that in common that
everyday things seem to them new and attractive.

FRIEDRICH NIETZSCHE

Art arises when the secret vision of the artist and
the manifestation of nature agree to find new shapes.

KAHLIL GIBRAN

Learning to draw is really a matter of learning
to see—to see correctly—and that means a good deal
more than merely looking with the eye.

KIMON NICOLAIDES

Drawing is the discipline by which I constantly rediscover the world. I have learned that what I have not drawn, I have never really seen, and that when I start drawing an ordinary thing, I realize how extraordinary it is, sheer miracle.

FREDERICK FRANCK

I shut my eyes in order to see.

PAUL GAUGUIN

Dancing is the loftiest, the most moving, the most beautiful of the arts, because it is no mere translation or abstraction from life; it is life itself.

HAVELOCK ELLIS

The body says what words cannot.

MARTHA GRAHAM

Dancing is the body made poetic.

ERNST BACON

The trouble with nude dancing is that
not everything stops when the music stops.

SIR ROBERT HELPMANN

Let that day be lost to us on which we did not dance once!

FRIEDRICH NIETZSCHE

If you can walk, you can dance.

ZIMBABWE SAYING

Music is well said to be the speech of angels.

THOMAS CARLYLE

Music is the child of prayer, the companion of religion.

CHATEAUBRIAND

Music is the art of the prophets, the only art that can calm
the agitations of the soul; it is one of the most magnificent
and delightful presents God has given us.

MARTIN LUTHER

Musical training is a more potent instrument
than any other, because rhythm and harmony
find their way into the inward places of the soul.

PLATO

We are full of rhythms . . . our pulse, our gestures,
our digestive tracts, the lunar and seasonal cycles.

YEHUDI MENUHIN

When I hear music, I fear no danger. I am invulnerable.
I see no foe. I am related to the earliest times, and to the latest.

HENRY DAVID THOREAU

The best, most beautiful, and most perfect way that we have
of expressing a sweet concord of mind to each other is by music.

JONATHAN EDWARDS

When words leave off, music begins.

HEINRICH HEINE

After silence that which comes nearest
to expressing the inexpressible is music.

ALDOUS HUXLEY

Music is the universal language of mankind.

HENRY WADSWORTH LONGFELLOW

There is no feeling, except the extremes of fear
and grief that does not find relief in music.

GEORGE ELIOT

Without music, life is a journey through a desert.

PAT CONROY

I merely took the energy it takes to pout and wrote some blues.

DUKE ELLINGTON

God respects me when I work, but loves me when I sing.

RABINDRANATH TAGORE

We all have music inside us, and can learn
how to get it out, one way or another.

FRANK WILSON

Poetry ennobles the heart and the eyes, and unveils the meaning of
all things upon which the heart and the eyes dwell. It discovers the
secret rays of the universe, and restores to us forgotten paradises.

EDITH SITWELL

To read a poem in January is as lovely
as to go for a walk in June.

JEAN PAUL

Poetry is something to make us wiser and better,
by continually revealing those types of beauty and truth,
which God has set in all men's souls.

JAMES RUSSELL LOWELL

The poem is a little myth of man's capacity of making his life
meaningful. And in the end, the poem is not a thing we see—it is,
rather, a light by which we may see—and what we see is life.

ROBERT PENN WARREN

Poetry is the utterance of deep and heartfelt truth.
The true poet is very near the oracle.

EDWARD HUBBELL CHAPIN

The poets are only the interpreters of the gods.

SOCRATES

Poetry is simply the most beautiful, impressive,
and widely effective mode of saying things.

MATTHEW ARNOLD

When power narrows the area of man's concern, poetry
reminds him of the richness and diversity of his existence.

JOHN F. KENNEDY

When you read and understand a poem, comprehending its
rich and formal meanings, then you master chaos a little.

STEPHEN SPENDER

There is as much dignity in tilling
a field as in writing a poem.

BOOKER T. WASHINGTON

You will find poetry nowhere unless
you bring some of it with you.

JOSEPH JOUBERT

Beauty

Beauty is in the eye of the beholder.

MARGARET HUNGERFORD

Some thoughts always find us young, and keep us so.
Such a thought is the love of the universal and eternal beauty.

RALPH WALDO EMERSON

Anyone who keeps the ability to see beauty never grows old.

FRANZ KAFKA

Let the beauty you love be what you do.
There are a thousand ways to kneel and kiss the earth.

RUMI

Beautiful is greater than Good, for it includes the Good.

GOETHE

The most natural beauty in the world is honesty
and moral truth. For all beauty is truth.

LORD SHAFTESBURY

To do the useful thing, to say the courageous thing,
to contemplate the beautiful thing:
that is enough for one man's life.

T. S. ELIOT

I'm tired of all the nonsense about beauty being only skin-deep.
That's deep enough. What do you want—an adorable pancreas?

JEAN KERR

The fountain of beauty is the heart, and every
generous thought illustrates the walls of your chamber.

FRANCIS QUARLES

Beauty as we feel it is something indescribable;
what it is or what it means can never be said.

GEORGE SANTAYANA

Things are beautiful if you love them.

JEAN ANOUILH

There is certainly no absolute standard of beauty.
That precisely is what makes its pursuit so interesting.

JOHN KENNETH GALBRAITH

A thing of beauty is a joy forever.

JOHN KEATS

**When your inner eyes open, you can find immense
beauty hidden within the inconsequential details of daily
life. When your inner ears open, you can hear the subtle,
lovely music of the universe everywhere you go.**

TIMOTHY RAY MILLER

**Though we travel the world over to find the beautiful,
we must carry it with us or we will not find it.**

RALPH WALDO EMERSON

Creativity

God is in the world, or nowhere, creating continually in us and around us. Insofar as man partakes of this creative process does he partake of the divine, of God, and that participation is his immortality . . . .

ALFRED NORTH WHITEHEAD

You were placed on this earth
to create, not to compete.

ROBERT ANTHONY

Every moment of your life is infinitely creative and the universe is endlessly bountiful. Just put forth a clear enough request, and everything your heart truly desires must come to you.

SHAKTI GAWAIN

There is no greater joy than that of feeling oneself a creator. The triumph of life is expressed by creation.

HENRI BERGSON

Creativity is a central source of meaning in our lives . . . most of the things that are interesting, important, and human are the results of creativity . . . when we are involved in it, we feel that we are living more fully than during the rest of life.

MIHALY CSIKSZENTMIHALYI

Creativeness often consists of merely
turning up what is already there.

BERNICE FITZ-GIBBON

A hunch is creativity trying to tell you something.

FRANK CAPRA

I saw an angel in the block of marble
and I just chiseled 'til I set him free.

MICHELANGELO

In creating, the only hard thing's to begin;
A grass-blade's no easier to make than an oak.

JAMES RUSSELL LOWELL

No matter how old you get, if you can keep the desire
to be creative, you're keeping the man-child alive.

JOHN CASSAVETES

It is the child in man that is the source of his uniqueness
and creativeness, and the playground is the optimal milieu
for the unfolding of his capacities.

ERIC HOFFER

Many times we will get more ideas and better ideas
in two hours of creative loafing than in eight hours at a desk.

WILFRED PETERSON

If you are seeking creative ideas, go out walking.
Angels whisper to a man when he goes for a walk.

RAYMOND INMAN

Family

Babies

Children

Parents

Grandparents

Friendship

The whole world is my family.

POPE JOHN XXIII

**To us, family means putting your arms
around each other and being there.**

BARBARA BUSH

**The happiest moments of my life have been the few
which I have passed at home in the bosom of my family.**

THOMAS JEFFERSON

The family with an old person in it possesses a jewel.

CHINESE SAYING

Babies are such a nice way to start people.

DON HEROLD

**Each time a new baby is born there is a possibility of reprieve.
Each child is a new being, a potential prophet, a new spiritual
prince, a new spark of light precipitated into the outer darkness.**

R. D. LAING

Every baby born into the world is a finer one than the last.

CHARLES DICKENS

The infant is music itself.

HAZRAT INAYAT KHAN

When the first baby laughed for the first time, the laugh broke into a thousand pieces and they all went skipping about, and that was the beginning of fairies.

J. M. BARRIE

A baby is God's opinion that life should go on.

CARL SANDBURG

Children are God's apostles, day by day
Sent forth to preach of love, and hope, and peace.

JAMES RUSSELL LOWELL

Every child comes with the message
that God is not yet discouraged of man.

RABINDRANATH TAGORE

Bringing a child into the world is the greatest act of hope there is.

LOUISE HART

Children are the world's most valuable
resource and its best hope for the future.

JOHN F. KENNEDY

Blessed be childhood, which brings down something of
heaven into the midst of our rough earthliness.

HENRI AMIEL

Children are the bridge to heaven.

PERSIAN PROVERB

We are given children to test us and make us more spiritual.

GEORGE WILL

One laugh of a child will make the holiest day more sacred still.

ROBERT G. INGERSOLL

Children are the true connoisseurs.
What's precious to them has no price—only value.

BEL KAUFMAN

There are no seven wonders of the world
in the eyes of a child. There are seven million.

WALT STREIGHTIFF

Children, like animals, use all their senses to discover the world.
Then artists come along and discover it the same way all over again.

EUDORA WELTY

The only artists for whom I would make way are—children.
For me the paintings of children belong side by side with
the works of the masters.

HENRY MILLER

Every child is an artist.
The problem is how to remain an artist once he grows up.

PABLO PICASSO

Every child is born a genius.

R. BUCKMINSTER FULLER

Why, a four-year-old child could understand this report.
Run out and find me a four-year-old child.

GROUCHO MARX

Adults are always asking little kids what they want to be when
they grow up—'cause they're looking for ideas.

PAULA POUNDSTONE

What do we teach our children? . . . We should say to each of them:
Do you know what you are? You are a marvel. You are unique . . .
You may become a Shakespeare, a Michelangelo, a Beethoven.
You have the capacity for anything.

PABLO CASALS

By giving children lots of affection, you can help fill them
with love and acceptance of themselves.
Then that's what they will have to give away.

WAYNE DYER

Teaching kids to count is fine,
but teaching them what counts is best.

BOB TALBERT

It is infinitely more useful for a child to hear a story told
by a person than by computer. Because the greatest part of the
learning experience lies not in the particular words of the story
but in the involvement with the individual reading it.

FRANK SMITH

The parents exist to teach the child, but also they must learn what the child has to teach them; and the child has a very great deal to teach them.

ARNOLD BENNETT

Grown men can learn from very little children for the hearts of little children are pure. Therefore, the Great Spirit may show to them many things which older people miss.

BLACK ELK

Children have a remarkable talent for not taking the adult world with the kind of respect we are so confident it ought to be given. To the irritation of authority figures of all sorts, children expend considerable energy in "clowning around." They refuse to appreciate the gravity of our monumental concerns, while we forget that if we were to become more like children our concerns might not be so monumental.

CONRAD HYERS

Youth! Stay close to the young, and a little rubs off.

ALAN JAY LERNER

Those who love the young best stay young longer.

EDGAR FRIEDENBERG

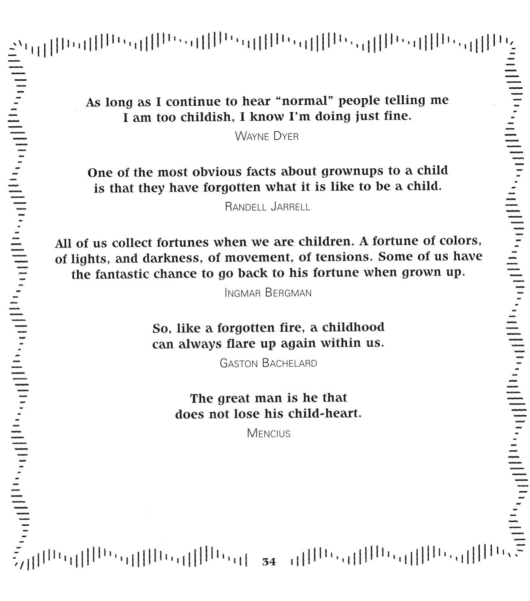

As long as I continue to hear "normal" people telling me
I am too childish, I know I'm doing just fine.

WAYNE DYER

One of the most obvious facts about grownups to a child
is that they have forgotten what it is like to be a child.

RANDELL JARRELL

All of us collect fortunes when we are children. A fortune of colors,
of lights, and darkness, of movement, of tensions. Some of us have
the fantastic chance to go back to his fortune when grown up.

INGMAR BERGMAN

So, like a forgotten fire, a childhood
can always flare up again within us.

GASTON BACHELARD

The great man is he that
does not lose his child-heart.

MENCIUS

What God is to the world, parents are to their children.

PHILO

Honor your father and your mother.

EXODUS 20:12

Honor your father and mother, even as you honor God,
for all three were partners in your creation.

ZOHAR

When I was a boy of fourteen, my father was so ignorant I could
hardly stand to have the old man around. But when I got to be
twenty-one, I was astonished at how much the old man had learned
in seven years.

MARK TWAIN

Remember, no matter how many candles you blow out this year,
there's one gal who will always think of you as young, strong
and handsome—your mother.

SUSAN D. ANDERSON

There's no way to be a perfect mother
and a million ways to be a good one.

JILL CHURCHILL

God could not be everywhere, therefore he made mothers.

JEWISH SAYING

Parents are often so busy with the physical rearing of children
that they miss the glory of parenthood, just as the grandeur
of the trees is lost when raking leaves.

MARCELENE COX

The best inheritance a parent can give his
children is a few minutes of his time each day.

O. A. BATTISTA

The simplest toy, one which even the youngest child
can operate, is called a grandparent.

SAM LEVENSON

If I had known how wonderful it would be to
have grandchildren, I'd have had them first.

LOIS WYSE

Few things are more delightful than grandchildren fighting over your lap.

DOUG LARSON

The greatest sweetener of human life is Friendship.

JOSEPH ADDISON

A friend might well be reckoned the masterpiece of nature.

RALPH WALDO EMERSON

Of all the things which wisdom provides to make us entirely happy,
much the greatest is the possession of friendship.

EPICURUS

Friendship is the only cement that will
ever hold the world together.

WOODROW WILSON

The glory of friendship is not the outstretched hand, nor the kindly
smile, nor the joy of companionship; it is the spiritual inspiration
that comes to one when he discovers that someone else
believes in him and is willing to trust him.

RALPH WALDO EMERSON

What a great blessing is a friend with a heart so trusty
you may safely bury all your secrets in it.

SENECA

When a friend is in trouble, don't annoy him by asking if there is
anything you can do. Think up something appropriate and do it.

EDGAR WATSON HOWE

A real friend is one who walks in when the rest of the world walks out.

WALTER WINCHELL

The most I can do for my friend is simply to be his friend.

HENRY DAVID THOREAU

Friendship improves happiness, and abates misery,
by doubling our joy, and dividing our grief.

JOSEPH ADDISON

It is not what you give your friend, but what you are willing
to give him, that determines the quality of your friendship.

MARY DIXON THAYER

A friend is someone who knows all
about you and loves you just the same.

ELBERT HUBBARD

It is not the talking that counts between friends,
it is the never needing to say what counts.

SHAWN GREEN

True friendship comes when silence
between two people is comfortable.

DAVE TYSON GENTRY

Friendship is a single soul dwelling in two bodies.

ARISTOTLE

To be a good friend remember that we are human magnets:
that like attracts like and that as we give we get.

WILFRED PETERSON

Treat your friends as you do your pictures,
and place them in their best light.

JENNIE JEROME CHURCHILL

Friendships are fragile things, and require as much care
in handling as any other fragile and precious thing.

RANDOLPH BOURNE

Every man should have a fair-sized cemetery
in which to bury the faults of his friends.

HENRY BROOKS ADAMS

Since there is nothing so well worth having as friends,
never lose a chance to make them.

FRANCESCO GUICCIARDINI

You can make more friends in two months by becoming more
interested in other people than you can in two years by trying
to get people interested in you.

DALE CARNEGIE

The only way to have a friend is to be one.

RALPH WALDO EMERSON

Friends will not only live in harmony, but in melody.

HENRY DAVID THOREAU

**It is great to have friends when one is young,
but indeed it is still more so when you are getting old.
When we are young, friends are, like everything else, a matter of
course. In the old days we know what it means to have them.**

EDVARD GRIEG

**Old friends are best. King James used to call for his old shoes;
they were the easiest for his feet.**

JOHN SELDEN

**Each of us has a spark of life inside us, and our highest endeavor
ought to be to set off that spark in one another.**

KENNY AUSUBEL

**Sometimes our light goes out but is blown into flame
by another human being. Each of us owes deepest thanks
to those who have rekindled this light.**

ALBERT SCHWEITZER

Heart

Blessed are the pure in heart, for they shall see God.

MATTHEW 5:8

The tiny flame that lights up the human heart is like a blazing torch
that comes down from heaven to light up the paths of mankind.
For in one soul are contained the hopes and feelings of all Mankind.

KAHLIL GIBRAN

Discouraged not by difficulties without, or the anguish of
ages within, the heart listens to a secret voice that whispers:
"Be not dismayed; in the future lies the Promised Land."

HELEN KELLER

When you wholeheartedly adopt a "with all your heart"
attitude and go all out with the positive principle,
you can do incredible things.

NORMAN VINCENT PEALE

When the heart of your heart opens, you can take deep pleasure
in the company of the people around you . . . When you are open
to the beauty, mystery, and grandeur of ordinary existence,
you "get it" that it always has been beautiful, mysterious,
and grand and always will be.

TIMOTHY RAY MILLER

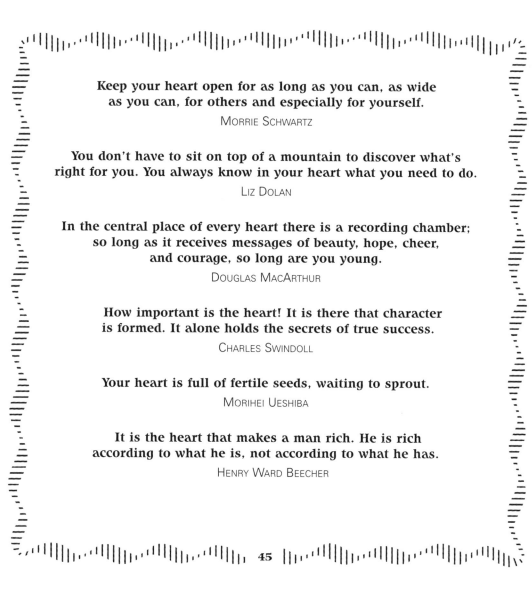

Keep your heart open for as long as you can, as wide
as you can, for others and especially for yourself.

MORRIE SCHWARTZ

You don't have to sit on top of a mountain to discover what's
right for you. You always know in your heart what you need to do.

LIZ DOLAN

In the central place of every heart there is a recording chamber;
so long as it receives messages of beauty, hope, cheer,
and courage, so long are you young.

DOUGLAS MACARTHUR

How important is the heart! It is there that character
is formed. It alone holds the secrets of true success.

CHARLES SWINDOLL

Your heart is full of fertile seeds, waiting to sprout.

MORIHEI UESHIBA

It is the heart that makes a man rich. He is rich
according to what he is, not according to what he has.

HENRY WARD BEECHER

In the rush of daily living it's easy to forget all the remarkable people, real or fictional, who have been a part of your life. But if you just imagine they are near for a moment, you will realize that anyone who ever touched your heart is always with you, patiently waiting to emanate warmth and support whenever you remember to think of them.

BARBARA SHER

May the blessing of light be on you, light without and light within.
May the blessed sunshine shine on you and warm your heart
till it glows like a great peat fire, so that the stranger
may come and warm himself at it, and also a friend.

IRISH BLESSING

Let us labor to make the heart grow larger as we become older,
as spreading oak gives more shelter.

RICHARD JEFFRIES

If wrinkles must be written upon our brows,
let them not be written upon the heart.
The spirit should not grow old.

JAMES A. GARFIELD

Great thoughts come from the heart.

LUC DE CLAPIERS

The best and most beautiful things in the world cannot
be seen or even touched. They must be felt with the heart.

HELEN KELLER

Trust your intuitive heart.

RICHARD CARLSON

What the heart knows today,
the head will understand tomorrow.

JAMES STEPHENS

It is only with the heart that one can see rightly;
what is essential is invisible to the eye.

ANTOINE DE SAINT-EXUPÉRY

47

Lighten Up

Cheerfulness

Smiles

Happiness

Humor

Play

Joy

Laughter

Love

A light heart lives long.

WILLIAM SHAKESPEARE

The one important thing I have learned over the years is the difference between taking one's work seriously and taking one's self seriously. The first is imperative and the second is disastrous.

MARGOT FONTEYN

Man, unlike the animal, has never learned that the sole purpose of life is to enjoy it.

SAMUEL BUTLER

There is no cure for birth or death save to enjoy the interval.

GEORGE SANTAYANA

Life's better when it's fun. Boy, that's deep, isn't it?

KEVIN COSTNER

When a man is gloomy, everything seems to go wrong; when he is cheerful, everything seems right!

PROVERBS 15:15

An ounce of cheerfulness is worth a
pound of sadness to serve God with.

THOMAS FULLER

Years back someone said cod liver oil was the cure-all!
Cheerfulness is more palliative and with no unpleasant aftertaste.

SR. MARY CHRISTELLE MACALUSO

Cheerfulness keeps up a kind of daylight in the mind,
filling it with a steady and perpetual serenity.

JOSEPH ADDISON

The highest wisdom is continual cheerfulness; such a state,
like the region above the moon, is always clear and serene.

MONTAIGNE

Let us be of good cheer, remembering that misfortunes
hardest to bear are those which never come.

JAMES RUSSELL LOWELL

Burdens become light when cheerfully borne.

OVID

A happy woman is one who has no cares at all; a cheerful woman
is one who has cares but doesn't let them get her down.

BEVERLY SILLS

Even if we can't be happy
we must always be cheerful.

IRVING KRISTOL

Nature intended you to be the fountain-spring
of cheerfulness and social life,
and not the mountain of despair and melancholy.

SIR ARTHUR HELPS

You find yourself refreshed by the presence
of cheerful people. Why not make an earnest effort
to confer that pleasure on others?
Half the battle is gained if you never allow yourself
to say anything gloomy.

LYDIA MARIA CHILD

Cheerfulness is contagious, but don't wait
to catch it from others. Be a carrier.

ANONYMOUS

If God came in and said, "I want you to be happy for the
rest of your life," what would you do?

BERNIE SIEGEL

True happiness is to understand our duties toward God and man;
to enjoy the present, without anxious dependence on the future;
not to amuse ourselves with either hopes or fears, but to rest satisfied
with what we have, which is abundantly sufficient.

SENECA

Many people think that if they were only in some other place, or had
some other job, they would be happy. Well, that is doubtful. So get
as much happiness out of what you are doing as you can and don't
put off being happy until some future date.

DALE CARNEGIE

You're happiest while you're making the greatest contribution.

ROBERT F. KENNEDY

The happiest and most contented people are those who
each day perform to make the best of their abilities.

ALFRED A. MONTAPERT

None but those who are happy in themselves can make others so.

WILLIAM HAZLITT

Do you want a world with . . . more joy and happiness? Then find your own joy and happiness and contribute to the joy and happiness of others.

BO LOZOFF

One thing I know; the only ones among you who will be really happy are those who will have sought and found how to serve.

ALBERT SCHWEITZER

Happiness is a perfume which you cannot pour on someone without getting some on yourself.

RALPH WALDO EMERSON

Remember that happiness is as contagious as gloom. It should be the first duty of those who are happy to let others know of their gladness.

MAURICE MAETERLINCK

Those who are happiest are those who do the most for others.

BOOKER T. WASHINGTON

Make people happy and there will not be half the quarreling, or a tenth part of the wickedness there now is.

LYDIA MARIA CHILD

Lead the life that will make you kindly and friendly to everyone about you, and you will be surprised what a happy life you will lead.

CHARLES SCHWAB

If you want to be happy, set yourself a goal that commands your thoughts, liberates your energy, and inspires your hopes. Happiness is within you. It comes from doing some certain thing into which you can put all your thought and energy. If you want to be happy, get enthusiastic about something.

DALE CARNEGIE

Happiness lies in the joy of achievement and the thrill of creative effort.

FRANKLIN D. ROOSEVELT

The way to happiness: keep your heart free from hate, your mind from worry. Live simply, expect little, give much. Fill your life with love. Scatter sunshine. Forget self, think of others. Do as you would be done by. Try this for a week and you will be surprised.

NORMAN VINCENT PEALE

The happiness of life is made up of minute fractions—the little, soon-forgotten charities of a kiss or smile, a kind look, a heartfelt compliment, and the countless infinitesimals of pleasurable and genial feeling.

SAMUEL TAYLOR COLERIDGE

A happy life is made up of little things . . .
a gift sent, a letter written, a call made, a recommendation given,
transportation provided, a cake made, a book lent, a check sent.

CAROL HOLMES

Do not worry; eat three square meals a day; say your prayers;
be courteous to your creditors; keep your digestion good; exercise;
go slow and easy. Maybe there are other things your special case
requires to make you happy, but my friend, these I reckon
will give you a good life.

ABRAHAM LINCOLN

The secret of happiness is this: Let your interests be as wide as possible,
and let your reactions to the things and persons that interest you
be as far as possible friendly rather than hostile.

BERTRAND RUSSELL

The secret of happiness is not in doing what one likes,
but in liking what one does.

J. M. BARRIE

The secret of happiness is to count your blessings
while others are adding up their troubles.

WILLIAM PENN

The secret of happiness is to count your
blessings—not your birthdays.

SHANNON ROSE

To be without some of the things you want
is an indispensable part of happiness.

BERTRAND RUSSELL

It is not how much we have, but how
much we enjoy, that makes happiness.

CHARLES SPURGEON

Before strongly desiring anything,
we should look carefully into the happiness of its present owner.

LA ROCHEFOUCAULD

We have all been placed on this earth to discover our own path,
and we will never be happy if we live someone else's idea of life.

JAMES VAN PRAAGH

The grand essentials to happiness in this life are something
to do, something to love, and something to hope for.

JOSEPH ADDISON

But what is happiness except the simple harmony
between a man and the life he leads.

ALBERT CAMUS

We all have 100% to deal with in our lives: 10% is important,
90% unimportant. The secret to a happy, productive life
is to deal with the 10% and let the 90% slip.

SALLI RASBERRY AND PADI SELWYN

With a little discipline and regular self-checks, you can learn to do
one thing at a time. And do it better. And be happier doing it.

ELAINE ST. JAMES

I've been riding the carousel in Central Park since I was five years old . . .
If I'm very depressed or if something's bothering me today, my husband,
Larry, and I go back to the park. We get on the carousel horse and we
start riding, and I start singing at the top of my lungs. It is pure and
absolute joy and happiness.

EDA LESHAN

It's never too late to have a happy childhood.

ANONYMOUS

Life holds so much, so much to be happy about always.
Most people ask for happiness on condition.
Happiness can be felt only if you don't set any conditions.

ARTUR RUBENSTEIN

Happiness is the spiritual experience of living
every minute with love, grace, and gratitude.

Denis Waitley

Better to be happy than wise.

John Heywood

Happiness is a butterfly, which, when pursued, is always just beyond
your grasp, but which, if you will sit down quietly, may alight upon you.

Nathaniel Hawthorne

Your success and happiness lie in you. Resolve to keep happy,
and your joy and you shall form an invisible host against difficulties.

Helen Keller

Remember that happiness is a way of travel, not a destination.

Roy Goodman

When ill luck besets us, to ease the tension we have only to
remember that happiness is relative. The next time you are tempted
to grumble about what has happened to you, why not pause and
be glad that it is no worse than it is?

Dale Carnegie

When one door of happiness closes, another opens; but often we look so long at the closed door that we do not see the one which has been opened for us.

HELEN KELLER

Many search for happiness as we look for a hat we wear on our heads.

NIKOLAUS LENUS

I have found that most people are about as happy as they make up their minds to be.

ABRAHAM LINCOLN

It is the happiness that comes from within that is lasting and fulfilling.

LEDDY SCHMELIGH

Each person on this planet is inherently, intrinsically capable of attaining "dizzying heights" of happiness and fulfillment.

WAYNE DYER

The ingredients of happiness are so simple that they can be counted on one hand. Happiness comes from within, and rests most securely on simple goodness and clear conscience.

WILLIAM OGDEN

We are never so happy nor so unhappy as we imagine.
LA ROCHEFOUCAULD

You have to believe in happiness, or happiness never comes.
DOUGLAS MALLOCH

It is a man's proper business to seek happiness and avoid misery.
JOHN LOCKE

The best way to secure future happiness
is to be as happy as is rightfully possible today.
CHARLES ELIOT

Why should we refuse the happiness this hour gives us,
because some other hour might take it away?
JOHN OLIVER HOBBES

At the end of our time on earth, if we have lived
fully, we will not be able to say, "I was always happy."
Hopefully, we will be able to say, "I have experienced a lifetime
of real moments, and many of them were happy moments."
BARBARA DEANGELIS

Cherish all your happy moments; they make a fine cushion for old age.
BOOTH TARKINGTON

Happiness is the meaning and the purpose of life,
the whole aim and end of human existence.

ARISTOTLE

The time to be happy is now. The place to be happy is here.

ROBERT G. INGERSOLL

Happiness and love are just a choice away.

LEO BUSCAGLIA

Our happiness depends on the habit of mind we cultivate.
So practice happy thinking every day. Cultivate the merry heart,
develop the happiness habit, and life will become a continual feast.

NORMAN VINCENT PEALE

Humor is the healthy way of feeling "distance" between one's self
and the problem, a way of standing off and looking
at one's problems with perspective.

ROLLO MAY

Humor has great power to heal on an emotional level.
You can't hold anger, you can't hold fear,
you can't hold hurt while you're laughing.

STEVE BHAERMAN
(A.K.A. SWAMI BEYONDANANDA)

Humor enables one to live in the midst of
tragic events without becoming a tragic figure.

E. T. "CY" EBERHART

There is no defense against adverse fortune which is
so effectual as an habitual sense of humor.

THOMAS HIGGINSON

Humor is our way of defending ourselves from life's
absurdities by thinking absurdly about them.

LEWIS MUMFORD

Common sense and a sense of humor are the same thing, moving at
different speeds. A sense of humor is just common sense, dancing.

CLIVE JAMES

There is always something to chuckle about. Sometimes we see it.
Sometimes . . . we don't. Still, the world is filled with humor.
It is there when we are happy and it is there to cheer us up when we are not.

ALLEN KLEIN

Joy is the most infallible sign of the Presence of God.

TEILHARD DE CHARDIN

Listen to the clues. The next time you feel real joy, stop and think. Pay attention. Because joy is the universe's way of knocking on your mind's door. Hello in there. Is anyone home? Can I leave a message? Yes? Good! The message is that you are happy, and that means that you are in touch with your purpose.

STEVE CHANDLER

Joy of life seems to me to arise from a sense of being where one belongs . . . of being foursquare with the life we have chosen. All the discontented people I know are trying sedulously to be something they are not, to do something they cannot do.

DAVID GRAYSON

When we align our thoughts, emotions, and actions with the highest part of ourselves, we are filled with enthusiasm, purpose, and meaning. . . . We are joyously and intimately engaged with our world. This is the experience of authentic power.

GARY ZUKAV

We have a tendency to obscure the forest of simple joys
with the trees of problems.

CHRISTIANE COLLANGE

People need joy quite as much as clothing. Some of them need it far more.

MARGARET COLLIER GRAHAM

When large numbers of people share their joy in common, the
happiness of each is greater because each adds fuel to the other's flame.

SAINT AUGUSTINE

Joys divided are increased.

JOSIAH GILBERT HOLLAND

You increase your joy by increasing the pure joy of others.

TORKOM SARAYDARIAN

Joy increases as you give it, and diminishes as you try
to keep it for yourself. In giving it, you will accumulate
a deposit of joy greater than you ever believed possible.

NORMAN VINCENT PEALE

As you express joy, you draw it out of those you meet,
creating joyful people and joyful events. The greater
the joy you express, the more joy you experience.

ARNOLD PATENT

When we feel joyful, euphoric, happy, we are more open to life,
more capable of seeing things clearly and handling daily tensions.

LEO BUSCAGLIA

If we could learn how to balance rest against effort, calmness
against strain, quiet against turmoil, we would assure ourselves
of joy in living and psychological health for life.

JOSEPHINE RATHBONE

Simplicity, clarity, singleness: these are the attributes
that give our lives power and vividness and joy.

RICHARD HALLOWAY

Joy is not in things; it is in us.

RICHARD WAGNER

Joy is the feeling of grinning on the inside.

MELBA COLGROVE

Joy is the will which labors, which overcomes obstacles,
which knows triumph.

WILLIAM BUTLER YEATS

It is in the compelling zest of high adventure and of victory,
and in creative action, that man finds his supreme joy.

ANTOINE DE SAINT-EXUPÉRY

I believe humans were born to have joy and to have it more abundantly; that the birthright of everyone is loving, caring, sharing, and abundance.

PETER MCWILLIAMS AND JOHN-ROGER

Joy is your birthright.

SARAH BAN BREATHNACH

Blessed are the joymakers.

NATHANIEL PARKER WILLIS

Laughter is the closest thing to the grace of God.

KARL BARTH

How to make God laugh: Tell him your future plans.

WOODY ALLEN

God is a comedian whose audience is afraid to laugh.

H. L. MENCKEN

Although a lot can be learned from adversity,
most of the same lessons can be learned
through laughter and joy.

PETER MCWILLIAMS

So when you're lonely or sad or bad or blue remember
where laughter's hiding . . . it's hiding inside of YOU!

DAVID SALTZMAN

Against the assault of laughter nothing can stand.

MARK TWAIN

In every job, relationship, or life situation there is inevitably some
turbulence. Learn to laugh at it. It is part of what you do and who you are.

ALLEN KLEIN

Laughter puts your brain, your central nervous system
and your whole being into a state of free play.

MAX EASTMAN

Laughing deeply is living deeply.

MILAN KUNDERA

It has always seemed to me that hearty laughter is
a good way to jog internally without having to go outdoors.

NORMAN COUSINS

A good belly laugh is like taking
your liver for a horseback ride.

BONNY CLARK

He laughs best whose laugh lasts.

LAURENCE J. PETER

Shared laughter is like throwing open the shutters in
a gloomy room and letting in fresh air and sunshine.

LILA GREEN

Laughter is the sun that drives winter from the human race.

VICTOR HUGO

Shared laughter is love made audible.

IZZY GESELL

A good laugh helps us recognize how ridiculous it is
to get excited about matters that are often trivial. . . .

ARTHUR ASA BERGER

Laughter is the brush that sweeps
away the cobwebs of the heart.

MORT WALKER

When we can laugh through out tears, we are being given a powerful message. Things may be bad, but they cannot be all that bad.

ALLEN KLEIN

The child in you, like all children, loves to laugh, to be around people who can laugh at themselves and life. Children instinctively know that the more laughter we have in our lives, the better.

WAYNE DYER

Laughter is a gift everyone should open.

GENE MITCHENER

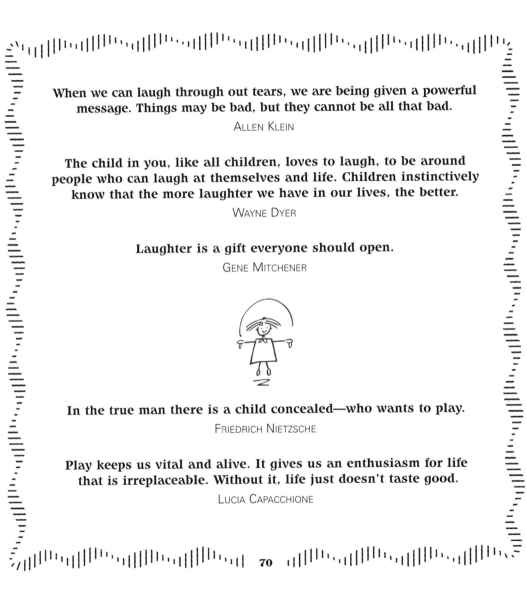

In the true man there is a child concealed—who wants to play.

FRIEDRICH NIETZSCHE

Play keeps us vital and alive. It gives us an enthusiasm for life that is irreplaceable. Without it, life just doesn't taste good.

LUCIA CAPACCHIONE

It's good to play, and you must keep in practice.

JERRY SEINFELD

The supreme accomplishment is to blur the line between work and play.

ARNOLD TOYNBEE

A little work, a little play,
To keep us going—and so, good-day!

GEORGE DU MAURIER

Get out of bed forcing a smile. You may not smile because you
are cheerful; but if you will force yourself to smile
you'll . . . be cheerful because you smile.

KENNETH GOODE

He who smiles rather than rages is always the stronger.

JAPANESE PROVERB

Every time a man smiles, and much more when
he laughs, it adds something to his fragment of life.

LAURENCE STERNE

What sunshine is to flowers, smiles are to humanity.
They are but trifles, to be sure; but, scattered along life's
pathway, the good they do is inconceivable.

JOSEPH ADDISON

It's easy enough to be pleasant when everything goes like a song,
but the man who is worthwhile, is the man who can smile,
when everything goes dead wrong.

ANONYMOUS

If you have made another person on this earth smile,
your life has been worthwhile.

SR. MARY CHRISTELLE MACALUSO

Wrinkles should merely indicate where smiles have been.

MARK TWAIN

Of all the things you wear, your expression is the most important.

JANET LANE

It is only through love that we can attain to communion with God.
All living knowledge of God rest upon this foundation:
that we experience Him in our lives as Will-to-love.

ALBERT SCHWEITZER

One word frees us of all the weight and pain
of life: That word is love.

SOPHOCLES

It makes no difference how deeply seated may be the trouble; how
hopeless the outlook; how muddled the tangle; how great the mistake.
A sufficient realization of love will dissolve it all. If only you could love
enough you would be the happiest and most powerful being in the world.

EMMET FOX

Love is the master key which opens the gates of happiness.

OLIVER WENDELL HOLMES, SR.

There is only one happiness in life, to love and be loved.
GEORGE SAND

Let no one who loves be called unhappy.
Even love unreturned has its rainbow.
J. M. BARRIE

What a grand thing, to be loved! What a grander thing still, to love!
VICTOR HUGO

To love and be loved is to feel the sun from both sides.
DAVID VISCOTT

Love . . . binds everything together in perfect harmony.
COLOSSIANS 3:14

For love . . . is the blood of life, the power of reunion in the separated.
PAUL TILLICH

It is this intangible thing, love in many forms, which enters into every
therapeutic relationship. . . . And it is an element which binds and
heals, which comforts and restores, which works what we have to
call—for now—miracles.
KARL MENNINGER

This is the miracle that happens every time to those
who really love; the more they give, the more they possess.

RAINER MARIA RILKE

The one thing we can never get enough of is love.
And the one thing we never give enough of is love.

HENRY MILLER

Love sought is good, but given unsought is better.

WILLIAM SHAKESPEARE

Don't shut love out of your life by saying it's impossible to find time.
The quickest way to receive love is to give; the fastest way to lose love
is to hold it too tightly; and the best way to keep love is to give it wings.

BRIAN DYSON

The love we give away is the only one we keep.

ELBERT HUBBARD

If you would be loved, love and be lovable.

BENJAMIN FRANKLIN

The issue is not so much being loved but being loving, which leads
to the same wonderful feeling you experience when someone loves you.

CAROL PEARSON

Everybody forgets the basic thing: people are
not going to love you unless you love them.

Pat Carroll

A loving person lives in a loving world. A hostile person
lives in a hostile world: everyone you meet is your mirror.

Ken Keyes, Jr.

Nine times out of ten, when you extend your arms to someone,
they will step in, because basically they need precisely what you need.

Leo Buscaglia

Love your enemies because they bring out the best in you.

Friedrich Nietzsche

Tolerance and celebration of individual
differences is the fire that fuels lasting love.

Tom Hannah

Do not waste time bothering whether you "love" your
neighbor; act as if you did. As soon as we do this we find
one of the great secrets. When you are behaving as if you
loved someone, you will presently come to love him.

C. S. Lewis

Thou shalt love thy neighbor as thyself.

LEVITICUS 19:18

**Love is a force that connects us to every strand of the universe,
an unconditional state that characterizes human nature, a form of
knowledge that is always there for us if only we can open ourselves to it.**

EMILY HILBURN SELL

**When we connect with ourselves in love,
we can connect with others and the planet in love.**

RATTANA HETZEL

Choose to be a love-finder rather than a faultfinder.

GERALD JAMPOLSKY

If you judge people, you have no time to love them.

MOTHER TERESA

**Someday, after we have mastered the winds, the waves, the tide
and gravity, we shall harness for God the energies of love. Then, for
the second time in the history of the world, man will have discovered fire.**

TEILHARD DE CHARDIN

Love keeps the cold out better than a cloak.

HENRY WADSWORTH LONGFELLOW

In the coldest February, as in every other month in every
other year, the best thing to hold on to in this world is each other.

LINDA ELLERBEE

True love always brings joy to ourself and to the one we love.
If our love does not bring joy to both of us, it is not true love.

THICH NHAT HANH

True love comes quietly, without banners or
flashing lights. If you hear bells, get your ears checked.

ERICH SEGAL

True love is night jasmine, a diamond in darkness, the heartbeat
no cardiologist has ever heard. It is the most common of miracles,
fashioned of fleecy clouds—a handful of stars tossed into the night sky.

JIM BISHOP

The essence of love is kindness.

ROBERT LOUIS STEVENSON

Love is what we were born with. Fear is what we learned here.

MARIANNE WILLIAMSON

Love is letting go of fear.

GERALD JAMPOLSKY

Love is much nicer to be in than an automobile accident, a tight girdle, a higher tax bracket, or a holding pattern over Philadelphia.

JUDITH VIORST

The Eskimos had fifty-two names for snow because it was important to them; there ought to be as many for love.

MARGARET ATWOOD

Every single one of us can do things that no one else can do—can love things that no one else can love . . . We are like violins. We can be used for doorstops, or we can make music.

BARBARA SHER

But some emotions don't make a lot of noise. It's hard to hear pride. Caring is real faint—like a heartbeat. And pure love—why, some days it's so quiet, you don't even know it's there.

ERMA BOMBECK

Love is not what we become but who we already are.

STEPHEN LEVINE

Ultimately, love is self-approval.

SONDRA RAY

Love is, above all, the gift of oneself.

JEAN ANOUILH

You must love yourself before you love another. By accepting
yourself and fully being what you are . . . your simple presence
can make others happy.

JANE ROBERTS

It is not what we do, it is how much love we put in the doing.

MOTHER TERESA

Forget the resolutions. Forget control and discipline . . . too much work.
Instead try experimenting. Go in search of something to fall in love with
. . . something about yourself, your career, your spouse.

DALE DAUTEN

Find something you love to do and you'll
never have to work a day in your life.

HARVEY MACKAY

You will find, as you look back upon your life,
that the moments when you really lived are the moments
when you have done things in the spirit of love.

HENRY DRUMMOND

We are most alive when we're in love.

JOHN UPDIKE

In our life there is a single color, as on an artist's palette,
which provides the meaning of life and art. It is the color of love.

MARC CHAGALL

Life is a flower of which love is the honey.

VICTOR HUGO

No one who has ever brought up a child can doubt for a moment
that love is literally the life-giving fluid of human existence.

SMILEY BLANTON

Anything will give up its secrets if you love it enough. Not only have I
found that when I talk to the little flower or to the little peanut they
will give up their secrets, but I have found that when I silently commune
with people they give up their secrets also—if you love them enough.

GEORGE WASHINGTON CARVER

A five-word sentence that could change the world tomorrow is
"What would love do now?"

NEALE DONALD WALSCH

Do not seek perfection in a changing world.
Instead, perfect your love.

MASTER SENGSTAN

Every day we are offered new means for learning and growing in love.

LEO BUSCAGLIA

Spend a moment, every day, thinking of someone to love.

RICHARD CARLSON

Ultimately love is everything.

M. SCOTT PECK

What the world really needs is more love and less paperwork.

PEARL BAILEY

Love doesn't make the world go 'round.
Love is what makes the ride worthwhile.

FRANKLIN P. JONES

Love is how you stay alive, even after you are gone.

MORRIE SCHWARTZ

Nature   Flowers

Gardens   Weather

New Day

God's miracles are to be found in nature itself;
the wind and waves, the wood that becomes a tree—all of these
are explained biologically, but behind them is the hand of God.

RONALD REAGAN

When I first open my eyes upon the morning meadows
and look out upon the beautiful world, I thank God I am alive.

RALPH WALDO EMERSON

If you wish to know the divine, feel the wind
on your face and the warm sun on your hand.

EIDO TAI SHIMANO ROSHI

The radiance in some places is so great as to be fairly dazzling . . .
every crystal, every flower a window opening into heaven,
a mirror reflecting the Creator.

JOHN MUIR

Nature is too thin a screen; the glory of
the omnipresent God bursts through everywhere.

RALPH WALDO EMERSON

I believe a leaf of grass is no less than the journey-work of the stars.

WALT WHITMAN

Look deep, deep into nature, and then you will
understand everything better.

ALBERT EINSTEIN

Come forth into the light of things. Let nature be your teacher.

WILLIAM WORDSWORTH

If you watch how nature deals with adversity,
continually renewing itself, you can't help but learn.

BERNIE SIEGEL

Rivers and rocks and trees have always been talking to us,
but we've forgotten how to listen.

MICHAEL ROADS

Contemplate the workings of this world. . . . Study how water flows in a
valley stream, smoothly and freely between the rocks . . . Everything—
even mountains, rivers, plants, and trees—should be your teacher.

MORIHEI UESHIBA

Speak to the earth, and it shall teach thee.

JOB 12:8

Adopt the pace of nature: her secret is patience.

RALPH WALDO EMERSON

Climb the mountains and get their good tidings: Nature's peace
will flow into you as sunshine into flowers, the winds will
blow their freshness into you, and the storms,
their energy and cares will drop off like autumn leaves.

JOHN MUIR

Nature tops the list of potent tranquilizers and stress reducers. The
mere sound of moving water has been shown to lower blood pressure.

PATCH ADAMS

The sun—my almighty physician.

THOMAS JEFFERSON

Nature uses only the longest threads to weave her patterns, so each
small piece of her fabric reveals the organization of the entire tapestry.

RICHARD FEYNMAN

The finest workers in stone are not copper or steel tools,
but the gentle touches of air and water working at their leisure
with a liberal allowance of time.

HENRY DAVID THOREAU

To the dull mind all nature is leaden. To the illumined
mind the whole world burns and sparkles with light.

RALPH WALDO EMERSON

The beauty of the world and the orderly arrangement of everything celestial makes us confess that there is an excellent and eternal nature, which ought to be worshiped and admired by all mankind.

CICERO

In all things of nature there is something of the marvelous.

ARISTOTLE

The sun gives us light, but the moon provides inspiration.
If you look at the sun without shielding your eyes, you'll go blind.
If you look at the moon without covering your eyes, you'll become a poet.

SERGE BOUCHARD

The world is full of poetry. The air is living with its spirit; and the waves dance to the music of its melodies, and sparkle in its brightness.

PERCIVAL

The sky is the daily bread of the eyes.

RALPH WALSO EMERSON

My heart leaps up when I behold a rainbow in the sky.

WILLIAM WORDSWORTH

The bluebird carries the sky on his back.

HENRY DAVID THOREAU

The clearest way into the Universe is through a forest wilderness.

JOHN MUIR

We lose our souls if we lose the experience of the forest, the butterflies, the song of the birds, if we can't see the stars at night.

THOMAS BERRY

Forget not that the earth delights to feel your bare feet and the winds long to play with your hair.

KAHLIL GIBRAN

As long as the Earth can make a spring every year, I can. As long as the Earth can flower and produce nurturing fruit, I can, because I'm the Earth. I won't give up until the Earth gives up.

ALICE WALKER

The creation of a thousand forests is in one acorn.

RALPH WALDO EMERSON

I never knew how soothing trees are—many trees and patches of open sunlight, and tree presences; it is almost like having another being.

D. H. LAWRENCE

Nature is saturated with deity.

RALPH WALDO EMERSON

Our Lord has written the promise of resurrection,
not in books alone but in every leaf of springtime.

MARTIN LUTHER

The nicest thing about the promise of spring
is that sooner or later she'll have to keep it.

MARK BELTAIRE

Spring is nature's way of saying, "Let's party!"

ROBIN WILLIAMS

It was one of those perfect summer days—the sun was shining, a breeze
was blowing, the birds were singing, and the lawnmower was broken.

JAMES DENT

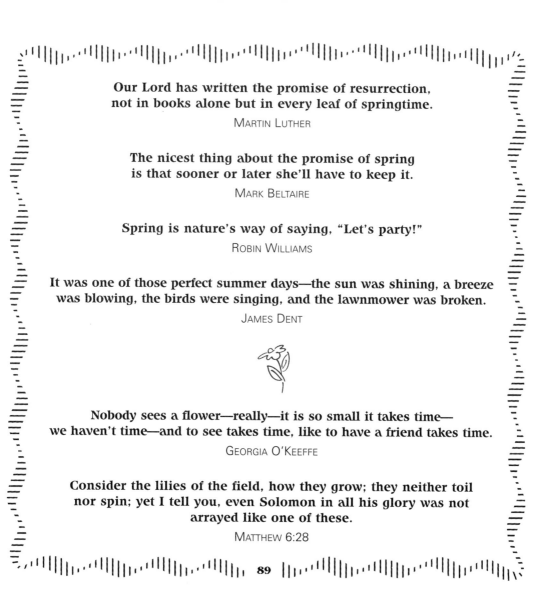

Nobody sees a flower—really—it is so small it takes time—
we haven't time—and to see takes time, like to have a friend takes time.

GEORGIA O'KEEFFE

Consider the lilies of the field, how they grow; they neither toil
nor spin; yet I tell you, even Solomon in all his glory was not
arrayed like one of these.

MATTHEW 6:28

The Amen! of Nature is always a flower.

OLIVER WENDELL HOLMES, SR.

Next time a sunrise steals your breath or a meadow of flowers leave you speechless, remain that way. Say nothing, and listen as heaven whispers, "Do you like it? I did it just for you."

MAX LUCADO

Every flower is a soul blossoming in Nature.

GÉRARD DE NERVAL

Flowers always make people better, happier, and more helpful; they are sunshine, food, and medicine to the soul.

LUTHER BURBANK

Earth laughs in flowers.

RALPH WALDO EMERSON

God Almighty first planted a garden. And indeed it is the purest of human pleasures.

FRANCIS BACON

Pleasure for an hour, a bottle of wine; pleasure for a year, marriage; pleasure for a lifetime, a garden.

CHINESE SAYING

The kiss of sun for pardon,
The song of the birds for mirth
One is nearer God's Heart in a garden
Than anywhere else on earth.

DOROTHY GURNEY

All gardeners live in beautiful places because they make them so.

JOSEPH JOUBERT

All gardening is landscape painting.

ALEXANDER POPE

What is a weed? A plant whose virtues have not yet been discovered.

RALPH WALDO EMERSON

For many years I was self-appointed inspector of snowstorms and rainstorms, and did my duty faithfully, though I never received one cent for it.

HENRY DAVID THOREAU

The next time it begins to rain . . . lie down on your belly, nestle your chin into the grass, and get a frog's-eye view of how raindrops fall . . . The sight of hundreds of blades of grass bowing down and popping back up like piano keys strikes me as one of the merriest sights in the world.

MALCOLM MARGOLIN

Sunshine is delicious, rain is refreshing, wind braces us up, snow is exhilarating; there is really no such thing as bad weather, only different kinds of good weather.

JOHN RUSKIN

Don't knock the weather; nine-tenths of the people couldn't start a conversation if it didn't change once in a while.

KIN HUBBARD

After rain comes fair weather.

JAMES HOWELL

Weather means more when you have a garden. There's nothing like listening to a shower and thinking how it is soaking in around your green beans.

MARCELENE COX

This is the day the Lord had made.
We will rejoice and be glad in it.

PSALMS 118:24

I have always been delighted at the prospect of a new day,
a fresh try, one more start, with perhaps a bit of magic
waiting somewhere behind the morning.

J. B. PRIESTLY

Whether one is twenty, forty, or sixty; whether one has succeeded,
failed or just muddled along; whether yesterday was full of sun or storm,
or one of those dull days with no weather at all, life begins each morning!

LEIGH MITCHELL HODGES

Today a new sun rises for me; everything lives,
everything is animated, everything seems to speak
to me of my passion, everything invites me to cherish it.

ANNE DE LENCLOS

Every new day begins with possibilities. It's up to us
to fill it with the things that move us toward progress and peace.

RONALD REAGAN

I love the challenge of starting at zero every day
and seeing how much I can accomplish.

MARTHA STEWART

Thank God ever morning when you get up that you have
something to do which must be done, whether you like it or not.

CHARLES KINGSLEY

Today is a new day. You will get out of it just what you put into it . . .
If you have made mistakes, even serious mistakes, there is always another
chance for you. . . . for this thing that we call "failure"
is not the falling down, but the staying down.

MARY PICKFORD

Finish each day and be done with it. You have done what you could;
some blunders and absurdities have crept in; forget them as soon as you
can. Tomorrow is a new day; you shall begin it serenely and with too
high a spirit to be encumbered with your old nonsense.

RALPH WALDO EMERSON

Live your life each day as you would climb a mountain.
An occasional glance toward the summit keeps the goal in mind,
but many beautiful scenes are to be observed from each new vantage point.
Climb slowly, steadily, enjoying each passing moment; and the view from
the summit will serve as a fitting climax for the journey.

HAROLD B. MELCHART

Nothing is worth more than this day.

GOETHE

Write it on your heart that every day is the best day in the year.

RALPH WALDO EMERSON

Normal day, let me be aware of the treasure you are.
Let me learn from you, love you, bless you before you depart.
Let me not pass you by in quest of some rare and perfect tomorrow.

MARY JEAN IRON

Yesterday is not ours to recover, but tomorrow is ours to win or lose.

LYNDON B. JOHNSON

When all else is lost, the future still remains.

CHRISTIAN BOVEE

When I look at the future, it's so bright, it burns my eyes.

OPRAH WINFREY

Time spent with cats is never wasted.
COLETTE

There are two means of refuge from the miseries of life: music and cats.
ALBERT SCHWEITZER

You can't look at a sleeping cat and be tense.
JANE PAULEY

**It is impossible to keep a straight face
in the presence of one or more kittens.**
CYNTHIA E. VARNADO

**Dogs come when they're called;
cats take a message and get back to you.**
MARY BLY

**Cats are smarter than dogs. You can't
get eight cats to pull a sled through snow.**
JEFF VALDEZ

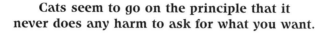

Cats seem to go on the principle that it
never does any harm to ask for what you want.

Joseph Wood Krutch

Cats are angels with fur.

Sark

Whoever said you can't buy happiness forgot about little puppies.

Gene Hill

There is no psychiatrist in the world like a puppy licking your face.

Bern Williams

Know thyself. Don't accept your dog's admiration
as conclusive evidence that you are wonderful.

Ann Landers

Dogs are not our whole life, but they make our lives whole.

Roger Caras

Living with a dog is one way to retain something of a child's spirit.

Michael Rosen

A dog is the only thing on earth
that loves you more than he loves himself.

JOSH BILLINGS

The greatest pleasure of a dog is that you may make a fool
of yourself with him, and not only will he not scold you,
but he will make a fool of himself, too.

SAMUEL BUTLER

The dog is the god of frolic.

HENRY WARD BEECHER

I wonder if other dogs think poodles
are members of a weird religious cult.

RITA RUDNER

I have always thought of a dog lover
as a dog that was in love with another dog.

JAMES THURBER

A dog wags its tail with its heart.

MARTIN BUXBAUM

Dogs laugh, but they laugh with their tails.

MAX EASTMAN

Money will buy a pretty good dog
but it won't buy the wag of his tail.

JOSH BILLINGS

No matter how little money and how few
possessions you own, having a dog makes you rich.

LOUIS SABIN

Peace is the first thing the angels sang. Peace is the mark of the sons
of God. Peace is the nurse of love. Peace is the mother of unity.
Peace is the rest of blessed souls. Peace is the dwelling place of eternity.

LEO THE GREAT

Peace is a daily, a weekly, a monthly process, gradually changing opinions,
slowly eroding old barriers, quietly building new structures. And however
undramatic the pursuit of peace, the pursuit must go on.

JOHN F. KENNEDY

Choose to experience peace rather than conflict.

Gerald Jampolsky

You don't have to have fought in a war to love peace.

Geraldine Ferraro

War is an invention of the human mind.
The human mind can invent peace.

Norman Cousins

I think that people want peace so much that one of these days
governments had better get out of their way and let them have it.

Dwight D. Eisenhower

If we have no peace, it is because we have forgotten
that we belong to each other.

Mother Teresa

Until he extends his circle of compassion to
all living things, man will not find peace.

Albert Schweitzer

It isn't enough to talk about peace; one must believe in it.
And it isn't enough to believe in it; one must work at it.

Eleanor Roosevelt

Before it's too late, and time is running out, let us turn from trust in the chain reactions of exploding atoms to faith of the chain reaction of God's love. Love—love of God and fellow men. That is God's formula for peace.

RICHARD CARDINAL CUSHING

The more we sweat in peace the less we bleed in war.

VIJAYA LAKSHMI PANDIT

It is understanding that gives us an ability to have peace. When we understand the other fellow's viewpoint, and he understands ours, then we can sit down and work out our differences.

HARRY S TRUMAN

It takes two to make peace.

JOHN F. KENNEDY

We merely want to live in peace with all the world, to trade with them, to commune with them, to learn from their culture as they may learn from ours, so that the products of our toil may be used for our schools and our roads and our churches and not for guns and planes and tanks and ships of war.

DWIGHT D. EISENHOWER

The place to improve the world is first in one's own heart and head and hands.

ROBERT PERSIG

If we have not peace within ourselves, it is
in vain to seek it from outward sources.

LA ROCHEFOUCAULD

The only way to bring peace to the earth
is to learn to make our own life peaceful.

THE BUDDHA

Peace, like charity, begins at home.

FRANKLIN D. ROOSEVELT

May you have warmth in your igloo, oil in your lamp,
and peace in your heart.

ESKIMO PROVERB

Positive thoughts (joy, happiness, fulfillment, achievement, worthiness) have positive results (enthusiasm, calm, well-being, ease, energy, love). Negative thoughts (judgment, unworthiness, mistrust, resentment, fear) produce negative results (tension, anxiety, alienation, anger, fatigue).

PETER MCWILLIAMS AND JOHN-ROGER

Could we change our attitude, we should not only see life differently, but life itself would come to be different. Life would undergo a change of appearance because we ourselves had undergone a change in attitude.

KATHERINE MANSFIELD

Life is a mirror and will reflect back to the thinker what he thinks into it.

ERNEST HOLMES

Our thoughts and imaginations are the only real limits to our possibilities.

ORISON S. MARDEN

It is the mind that maketh good of ill, that maketh wretch or happy, rich or poor.

EDMUND SPENSER

Most of us can, as we choose, make of this
world either a palace or a prison.

SIR JOHN LUBBOCK

We are each gifted in a unique and important way. It is our
privilege and our adventure to discover our own special light.

MARY DUNBAR

Before a painter puts a brush to his canvas he sees his picture
mentally. . . . If you think of yourself in terms of a painting, what do
you see? . . . Is the picture one you think worth painting? . . . You
create yourself in the image you hold in your mind.

THOMAS DREIER

We cannot tell what may happen to us in the strange medley of life.
But we can decide what happens in us—how we take it,
what we do with it—and that is what really counts in the end.

JOSEPH NEWTON

Get into the habit of looking for the silver lining of the cloud, and,
when you have found it, continue to look at it, rather than at the
leaden gray in the middle. It will help you over many hard places.

A. A. WILLITTS

Keep your face to the sunshine and you cannot see the shadow.

HELEN KELLER

There is very little difference in people, but that little
difference makes a big difference. The little difference is
attitude. The big difference is whether it is positive or negative.

W. CLEMENT STONE

It is not the situation. It is your reaction to the situation.

BOB CONKLIN

There are two big forces at work, external and internal. We have very
little control over external forces such as tornadoes, earthquakes, floods,
disasters, illness, and pain. What really matters is the internal force. How
do I respond to those disasters? Over that I have complete control.

LEO BUSCAGLIA

If you will call your troubles experiences, and remember that every
experience develops some latent force within you, you will grow vigorous
and happy, however adverse your circumstances may seem to be.

JOHN MILLER

Diseases can be our spiritual flat tires—disruptions in our lives
that seem to be disasters at the time but end by redirecting
our lives in a meaningful way.

BERNIE SIEGEL

Out of difficulties grow miracles.

LA BRUYÉRE

Great emergencies and crises show us how much
greater our vital resources are than we had supposed.

WILLIAM JAMES

In the depth of winter I finally learned
that there was in me an invincible summer.

ALBERT CAMUS

God gave us our memories so that we might have roses in December.

J. M. BARRIE

I'm not afraid of storms for I'm learning how to sail my ship.

LOUISA MAY ALCOTT

Help us to be the always hopeful gardeners of the spirit who know that
without darkness nothing comes to birth as without light nothing flowers.

MAY SARTON

The quickest way to change your attitude toward pain
is to accept the fact that everything that happens to us
has been designed for our spiritual growth.

M. SCOTT PECK

When somebody is angry with us, we draw a halo around his or her head, in our minds. Does the person stop being angry then? Well, we don't know! We know, though, that when we draw a halo around a person, suddenly the person starts to look like an angel to us.

JOHN LENNON AND YOKO ONO

Picture yourself placing your problem inside a pale, yellow balloon, letting it go, watching it drift until it is a tiny pastel dot in the sky.

BARBARA MARKOFF

Whenever something good happens, write it down. Buy a special notebook . . . and use it to list all the good in your life.

PETER MCWILLIAMS AND JOHN-ROGER

It doesn't hurt to be optimistic. You can always cry later.

LUCIMAR SANTOS DE LIMA

The average pencil is seven inches long, with just a half-inch eraser—in case you thought optimism was dead.

ROBERT BRAULT

Pessimism never won any battle.

DWIGHT D. EISENHOWER

Stop the mindless wishing that things would be different. Rather than wasting time and emotional and spiritual energy in explaining why we don't have what we want, we can start to pursue other ways to get it.

GREG ANDERSON

Man is so made that whenever anything fires his soul, impossibilities vanish.

JEAN DE LA FONTAINE

Deep within man dwell those slumbering powers; powers that would astonish him, that he never dreamed of possessing; forces that would revolutionize his life if aroused and put into action.

ORISON S. MARDEN

Within you right now is the power to do things you never dreamed possible. This power becomes available to you just as soon as you can change your beliefs.

MAXWELL MALTZ

Exhilaration of life can be found only with an upward look. This is an exciting world. It is cram-packed with opportunity. Great moments wait around every corner.

RICHARD DEVOS

Enthusiasm is the greatest asset in the world. It beats money and power and influence.

HENRY CHESTER

Nothing splendid has ever been achieved except by those who dared
to believe that something inside of them was superior to circumstance.

BRUCE BARTON

It is the ultimate wisdom of the mountains that we are never
so much human as when we are striving for what is beyond our
grasp, and that there is no battle worth the winning save that
against our own ignorance and fear.

JAMES RAMSEY ULLMAN

I keep the telephone of my mind open to peace, harmony, health, love,
and abundance. Then whenever doubt, anxiety, or fear try to call me,
they keep getting a busy signal and soon they'll forget my number.

EDITH ARMSTRONG

You can do anything you wish to do, have anything
you wish to have, be anything you wish to be.

ROBERT COLLIER

People become really quite remarkable when they start
thinking that they can do things. When they believe
in themselves they have the first secret of success.

NORMAN VINCENT PEALE

What lies behind us and what lies before us
are small matter compared to what lies within us.

RALPH WALDO EMERSON

No matter what level of your ability, you have
more potential than you can ever develop in a lifetime.

JAMES McCAY

Everyone has got it in him, if he will only make up his
mind and stick at it. None of us is born with a stop-valve on
his powers or with a set limit to his capacities. There is no
limit possible to the expansion of each one of us.

CHARLES SCHWAB

Everyone has inside of him a piece of good news. The good
news is that you don't know how great you can be! How much you
can love! What you can accomplish! And what your potential is!

ANNE FRANK

The power which resides in man is new in nature,
and none but he knows what that is which he can do,
nor does he until he has tried.

RALPH WALDO EMERSON

Ask, and it shall be given you; seek, and ye shall find;
knock, and it shall be opened unto you.
For every one that asketh, receiveth; and he that seeketh, findeth;
and to him that knocketh it shall be opened.

MATTHEW 7:7, 8

Trust yourself.
You know more than you think you do.

BENJAMIN SPOCK

If we did all the things we are capable of doing,
we would literally astound ourselves.

THOMAS ALVA EDISON

Each of us makes his own weather, determines the color of the skies
in the emotional universe which he inhabits.

BISHOP FULTON J. SHEEN

Every beauty and greatness in this world is created by a single
thought or emotion inside a man. Every thing we see today,
made by past generations, was, before its appearance, a thought
in the mind of a man or an impulse in the heart of a woman.

KAHLIL GIBRAN

Be brave enough to live creatively. The creative is the place where
no one else has ever been. You have to leave the city of your comfort
and go into the wilderness of your intuition. You cannot get there by
bus, only by hard work, risking and by not quite knowing what you
are doing. What you will discover will be wonderful: yourself.

ALAN ALDA

Be not afraid of life. Believe that life is worth
living, and your belief will help create the fact.

WILLIAM JAMES

Your living is determined not so much by what life
brings to you as by the attitude you bring to life.

JOHN MILLER

I am not discouraged, because every wrong
attempt discarded is another step forward.

THOMAS ALVA EDISON

What is defeat? Nothing but education,
nothing but the first step toward something better.

WENDELL PHILLIPS

To every disadvantage there is a corresponding advantage.

W. CLEMENT STONE

Look at everything as though you were seeing it either for the first
or last time. Then your time on earth will be filled with glory.

BETTY SMITH

One for whom the pebble has value must be
surrounded by treasures wherever he goes.

PAR LAGERKVIST

We're all only fragile threads, but what a tapestry we make.

JERRY ELLIS

Today, let's give thanks for life.
For life itself. For simply being born!

DAPHNE ROSE KINGMA

Spirituality

Faith

Prayer

God

Soul

When I use the word spirituality, I don't necessarily mean religion;
I mean whatever it is that helps you feel connected
to something that is larger than yourself.

DEAN ORNISH

The spiritual life does not remove us from the world
but leads us deeper into it.

HENRI J. M. NOUWEN

The fact that I can plant a seed and it becomes a flower, share
a bit of knowledge and it becomes another's, smile at someone
and receive a smile in return, are to me continual spiritual exercises.

LEO BUSCAGLIA

Faith is the evidence of things not seen.

1 HEBREWS 11:1

They understand but little who understand only what can be explained.

MARIE EBNER-ESCHENBACH

Some things have to be believed to be seen.
RALPH HODGSON

Faith is like electricity. You can't see it, but you can see the light.
ANONYMOUS

**Faith is the strength by which a shattered world
shall emerge into the light.**
HELEN KELLER

Live your beliefs and you can turn the world around.
HENRY DAVID THOREAU

**If you can't have faith in what is held up to you for faith,
you must find things to believe in yourself, for life
without faith in something is too narrow a space to live.**
GEORGE EDWARD WOODBERRY

I am one of those who would rather sink with faith than swim without it.
STANLEY BLADWIN

**If a blade of grass can grow in a concrete walk and a fig tree in the side
of a mountain cliff, a human being empowered with an invincible faith
can survive all odds the world can throw against his tortured soul.**
ROBERT H. SCHULLER

Faith is not knowledge of what the mystery of the universe is, but the conviction that there is a mystery, and that it is greater than us.

RABBI DAVID WOLPE

Faith is our direct link to universal wisdom, reminding us that we know more than we have heard or read or studied— that we have only to look, listen, and trust the love and wisdom of the Universal Spirit working through us all.

DAN MILLMAN

Believe in something larger than yourself.

BARBARA BUSH

Faith is knowing there is an ocean because you have seen a brook.

WILLIAM ARTHUR WARD

Faith is, above all, openness; an act of trust in the unknown.

ALAN WATTS

Faith is believing before receiving.

ALFRED A. MONTAPERT

Faith is not being sure where you're going but going anyway.

FREDRICK BUECHNER

**Faith is to believe what we do not see;
the reward of this faith is to see what we believe.**

SAINT AUGUSTINE

You can do very little with faith, but you can do nothing without it.

SAMUEL BUTLER

All things are possible to him who believes.

MARK 9:23

**Faith is the bird that feels the light
and sings when the dawn is still dark.**

RABINDRANATH TAGORE

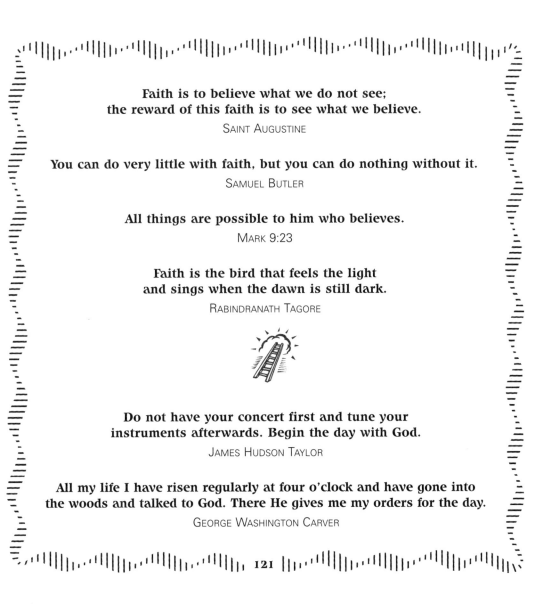

**Do not have your concert first and tune your
instruments afterwards. Begin the day with God.**

JAMES HUDSON TAYLOR

**All my life I have risen regularly at four o'clock and have gone into
the woods and talked to God. There He gives me my orders for the day.**

GEORGE WASHINGTON CARVER

The strength of a man consists in finding out the
way in which God is going, and going in that way too.

HENRY WARD BEECHER

God gives us always strength enough, and sense
enough, for everything He wants us to do.

JOHN RUSKIN

God gave burdens, also shoulders.

JEWISH SAYING

There is literally nothing that I ever asked to do,
that I asked the blessed Creator to help me
to do, that I have not been able to accomplish.

GEORGE WASHINGTON CARVER

Here on earth, God's work must surely be our own.

JOHN. F. KENNEDY

God can dream a bigger dream for you than you can dream
for yourself, and your role on Earth is to attach yourself
to that divine force and let yourself be released to it.

OPRAH WINFREY

We were born to make manifest the glory of God that is within us. It's not just in some of us, it's in everyone.

NELSON MANDELA

I believe God is managing affairs and that He doesn't need any advice from me. With God in charge, I believe everything will work out for the best in the end.

HENRY FORD

In a world filled with causes for worry and anxiety . . . we need the peace of God standing guard over our hearts and minds.

JERRY MCCANT

Remember that everything has God's fingerprints on it.

RICHARD CARLSON

There is not a flower that opens, not a seed that falls into the ground, and not an ear of wheat that nods on the end of its stalk in the wind that does not preach and proclaim the greatness and the mercy of God to the whole world.

THOMAS MERTON

Millions of angels are at God's command.

BILLY GRAHAM

The Holy Spirit . . . wants to flow through us and realize
all these wonderful possibilities in the world—if we only open
ourselves and allow it to happen.

BR. DAVID STEINDL-RAST

Do you not know that you are God's temple
and that God's spirit dwells within you?

1 CORINTHIANS 3:16

God does not ask your ability, or your inability.
He asks only your availability.

MARY KAY ASH

When you have succeeded in enshrining God
within your heart, you will see Him everywhere.

SWAMI SHIVANANDA

God dwells wherever man lets Him in.

JEWISH SAYING

God is love.

1 JOHN 4:8

God loves you. God doesn't want anyone to be hungry and oppressed. He
just puts his big arms around everybody and hugs them up against himself.

NORMAN VINCENT PEALE

God loves us the way we are but He
loves us too much to leave us that way.

LEIGHTON FORD

The best minister is the human heart; the best teacher is time;
the best book is the world; the best friend is God.

JEWISH SAYING

I love God, and when you get to know Him, you find He's a Livin' Doll.

JANE RUSSELL

I don't believe in God. Just try getting a plumber on the weekend.

WOODY ALLEN

God comes at last when we think he is farthest off.

JAMES HOWELL

God gave you a gift of 86,400 seconds today.
Have you used one to say "thank you"?

WILLIAM ARTHUR WARD

If you begin to live life looking for the God that is
all around you, every moment becomes a prayer.

FRANK BIANCO

A single grateful thought toward heaven is the most complete prayer.

GOTTHOLD EPHRAIM LESSING

Prayer may not change things for you,
but it for sure changes you for things.

SAMUEL SHOEMAKER

Get down on your knees and thank God you are on your feet.

IRISH SAYING

Time spent on the knees in prayer will do more to remedy
heart strain and nerve worry than anything else.

GEORGE DAVID STEWART

You pray in your distress and in your need; would that you might pray also in the fullness of your joy and in your days of abundance.

KAHLIL GIBRAN

I never went to bed in my life and I never ate a meal in my life without saying a prayer. I know my prayers have been answered thousands of times, and I know that I never said a prayer in my life without something good coming of it.

JACK DEMPSEY

God answers all our prayers. Sometimes the answer is yes. Sometimes the answer is no. Sometimes the answer is, you've got to be kidding!

JIMMY CARTER

Why is it when we talk to God we are said to be praying, and when God talks to us we're said to be schizophrenic?

LILY TOMLIN

A grandfather was walking through his yard when he heard his granddaughter repeating the alphabet in a tone of voice that sounded like a prayer. He asked her what she was doing. The little girl explained: "I'm praying, but I can't think of exactly the right words, so I'm just saying all the letters, and God will put them together for me, because He knows what I'm thinking."

CHARLES B. VAUGHAN

When you recover or discover something that nourishes your soul and brings joy, care enough about yourself to make room for it in your life.

JEAN SHINODA BOLEN

It's important to be heroic, ambitious, productive, efficient, creative, and progressive, but these qualities don't necessarily nurture the soul. The soul has different concerns, of equal value: downtime for reflection, conversation, and reverie; beauty that is captivating and pleasuring; relatedness to the environs and to people; and any animal's rhythm of rest and activity.

THOMAS MOORE

Excite the soul, and the weather and the town and your condition in the world all disappear; the world itself loses its solidity, nothing remains but the soul and the Divine Presence in which it lives.

RALPH WALDO EMERSON

The soul is awakened through service.

ERICA JONG

Souls are made of dawn-stuff and starshine.

ELBERT HUBBARD

I was thrown out of college for cheating on the metaphysics exam; I looked into the soul of the boy next to me.

WOODY ALLEN

Nobody grows old by merely living a number of years. People grow old only by deserting their ideals. Years wrinkle the face, but to give up enthusiasm wrinkles the soul.

WATTERSON LOWE

The purpose of life on earth is that the soul should grow— So Grow! By doing what is right.

ZELDA FITZGERALD

The soul . . . is audible, not visible.

HENRY WADSWORTH LONGFELLOW

Soul appears when we make room for it.

THOMAS MOORE

Wealth

True abundance is not about gathering more things, it's about
touching the place in us that is connected to the divine source of
abundance, so that we know what we need in the moment will be provided.

MARY MANIN MORRISSEY

It's time we put thoughts of lack behind us. It's time for us
to discover the secrets of the stars, to sail to an uncharted land,
to open up a new heaven where our spirits can soar.

SARAH BAN BREATHNACH

It is good to have things that money can buy, but it is also good to
check up once in awhile and be sure we have the things money can't buy.

GEORGE HORACE LORIMER

Ordinary riches can be stolen, real riches cannot. In your soul are
infinitely precious things that cannot be taken from you.

OSCAR WILDE

Let us not get so busy or live so fast that we can't listen to
the music of the meadow or the symphony that glorifies the forest.
Some things in the world are far more important than wealth;
one of them is the ability to enjoy simple things.

DALE CARNEGIE

It is wealth to be content.

Lao-Tzu

Who is rich? He that rejoices in his portion.

Benjamin Franklin

If you're happy, you're wealthy! Happiness doesn't need a bank account.

Sr. Mary Christelle Macaluso

Wealth . . . is a relative thing since he that has little and wants less is richer than he that has much but wants more.

Charles Caleb Colton

Sometimes when you have everything, you can't really tell what matters.

Christina Onassis

The only question with wealth is what you do with it.

John D. Rockefeller, Jr.

The rich man is not one who is in possession of much, but one who gives much.

Saint John Chrysostom

Having given all he had,
He then is very rich indeed.

LAO-TZU

If you see yourself as prosperous, you will be.
If you see yourself as continually hard up,
that is exactly what you will be.

ROBERT COLLIER

Prosperity is just around the corner.

HERBERT HOOVER

Wealth is not his that has it, but his who enjoys it.

BENJAMIN FRANKLIN

**Colors fade, temples crumble,
empires fall, but wise words endure.**

EDWARD THORNDIKE

Index

Eliot, T. S. 21
Ellerbee, Linda 78
Ellington, Duke 16
Ellis, Havelock 13
Ellis, Jerry 115
Emerson, Ralph Waldo 9, 20, 22, 37,
    38, 41, 54, 84, 85, 86, 87, 88, 90,
    91, 94, 95, 111, 112, 128
Epicurus 37
Exodus 35

F

Fadiman, Dorothy 11
Farrell, Joseph 8
Ferraro, Geraldine 102
Feynman, Richard 86
Fitz-Gibbon, Bernice 25
Fitzgerald, Zelda 129
Fonteyn, Margot 50
Ford, Henry 123
Ford, Leighton 125
Fox, Emmet 73
Franck, Frederick 13
Frank, Anne 112
Franklin, Benjamin 75, 133, 134
Friedenberg, Edgar 33
Fuller, R. Buckminster 31
Fuller, Thomas 51

G

Galbraith, John Kenneth 21
Garfield, James A. 46
Gauguin, Paul 13

Gawain, Shakti 24
Gentry, Dave Tyson 39
Gesell, Izzy 69
Gibran, Kahlil 12, 44, 88, 113, 127
Goethe 11, 20, 95
Goldwyn, Samuel 8
Goode, Kenneth 71
Goodman, Roy 59
Graham, Billy 123
Graham, Margaret Collier 65
Graham, Martha 13
Grayson, David 64
Green, Lila 69
Green, Shawn 39
Grieg, Edvard 41
Guicciardini, Francesco 40
Gurney, Dorothy 91

H

Haley, Alex 9
Halloway, Richard 66
Hanh, Thich Nhat 78
Hannah, Tom 76
Hart, Louise 30
Hawthorne, Nathaniel 59
Hazlitt, William 54
Heine, Heinrich 15
Helpmann, Sir Robert 14
Helps, Sir Arthur 52
Herold, Don 28
Hetzel, Rattana 77
Heywood, John 59
Higginson, Thomas 63
Hill, Gene 99

ABOUT THE AUTHOR

Allen Klein is an award-winning professional speaker and best-selling author. He teaches people worldwide how to use humor to deal with not-so-funny stuff. In addition to this book, Klein is also the author of *Quotations to Cheer You Up When the World is Getting You Down, Up Words for Down Days,* and *The Change-Your-Life Quote Book.*

For more information about Klein or his presentations go to www.allenklein.com, E-mail him at Author@allenklein.com, or write to him at 1034 Page Street, San Francisco, CA 94117.